# SIMPLE FARE FOR SICK FOLK

# SIMPLE FARE FOR SICK FOLK

RECIPES FOR FEEDING INVALIDS AND
CONVALESCENTS

COMPILED BY

## MAY BYRON

.

LONDON
HODDER & STOUGHTON LIMITED
1934

*Made and Printed in Great Britain for Hodder & Stoughton Limited, by Wyman & Sons Limited, London, Reading and Fakenham*

# CONTENTS

vii

# INTRODUCTION

DIETARY plays a much more conspicuous part, nowadays, in any variety of illness and convalescence than was ever thought of in former days. In such households as are, to speak plainly, survivals of the unfittest (and it is surprising to find how many such there are), there is little knowledge of any special fare for sick folk. Still less is there any knowledge of what may be specially *inadvisable* for certain cases. There were certain possets, caudles, broths, and gruels, certain " teas " and cooling drinks were provided. But the real regard to *suitable* and *palatable* diet is of comparatively recent growth.

I have endeavoured to provide here sufficient recipes to make things easier both for the patient and the cook. But a few extra suggestions will be found helpful, as follows :—

(1) Never be without some means of obtaining, at a few minutes' notice, boiling hot

9

water. A hot drink may quite probably assist in saving the patient's life, especially if it be coupled with a hot-water bottle. Heat to the feet—and to the navel as well, if possible—and heat to the stomach, by dint of hot water or tea, are often more important than food—anyhow, quicker in action. If you haven't a gas-ring, an oil-stove, a methylated-spirit lamp, you are in a very bad way. For an ordinary fire takes long to burn up ; a kettle takes long to boil ; and an old type of oil-stove may be slow in action. Yet I have known people in their eighties, without any means of obtaining or applying heat ! Not for want of money ; merely for lack of forethought.

(2) Daintiness is of much importance in serving food to a sick person. An elaborate tray-cloth and silver spoons will not " minister to a mind diseased," or to a body in miserable state. But everything should be *clean*, however homely. A cup of tea should not be splashed all over the saucer. Little careless, clumsy things which pass unnoticed in health may be positively distressful in sickness. Cleanness and tidiness (without being fussy),

have a good effect upon the patient's mind which can hardly be over-rated.

(3) Be sure that the patient is in a comfortable *attitude*, well arranged with pillows, etc. No trouble is too great to take where a sick person is concerned. But plenty of people imagine that any slapdash method will do. They are quite unable to put themselves in the place of the patient. Whether this comes from sheer stupidity, or from want of imagination, I do not know. But the result is the same.

(4) Do not leave soiled cups and glasses, etc., in a sick-room. Get them out of it as soon as may be. Whenever you are leaving a room, and going downstairs, have a good look round and see if there is nothing you can take with you. This may sound like ordinary common sense. But precious few people seem to possess it.

(5) Never bring a sick person tepid, lukewarm food or drink. This puts them off the food or drink at once. Let everything be " hot and hot " (unless, of course, a cold drink is essential). And do not repeat the same food—*variety* is most important. For

this reason, a small quantity of food, newly prepared and cooked, is much better than a large quantity re-heated and repeated until it is all used up.

(6) There are so many little odds and ends, of which only a person who has passed through many sicknesses could know, and about some of which, even a trained nurse might be unaware, that I must perforce omit them. But there is one point so important that it should be remembered continually ; and that applies especially to the mother, daughter, friend, maid, or whoever undertakes the cookery indicated in this book. That is PUNCTUALITY. A weak, ailing person in bed, if kept waiting too long for his or her food, may become almost past partaking of it. To serve a meal, however meagre, with strict *punctuality*, is a matter whose importance can scarcely be exaggerated. *Never keep your patient waiting.*

# WEIGHTS AND MEASURES

NOTE.—Roughly speaking, 1 pint of liquid (2 breakfast-cups) equals 1 pound of solid or dry material ; but this is not always quite accurate, and in the case of fruit and vegetables, a pint-measure is not always equivalent to a pound ; it may be so with small berries, nuts, etc., and with peas and beans ; but most vegetables are better bought by weight, not by measure.

## WEIGHTS AND MEASURES : *Liquid*

(*Cup* always means breakfast-cup.)

| | |
|---|---|
| 2 saltspoonfuls - - - | = 1 coffeespoonful. |
| 2 coffeespoonfuls or 55 drops | = 1 teaspoonful. |
| 4 teaspoonfuls - - - | = 1 tablespoonful, or $\frac{1}{2}$ oz. |
| 4 tablespoonfuls - - | = $\frac{1}{2}$ cup, or $\frac{1}{4}$ pint. |
| $\frac{1}{2}$ cup, or 8 large tablespoonfuls - - - - | = 1 gill. |

2 gills - - - - = 1 cup, or ½ pint.
2 cups, or 52 tablespoonfuls = 1 pint.
4 cups (2 pints) - - = 1 quart.
4 quarts (6 bottles) - - = 1 gallon.


## Weights and Measures : *Solid or Dry*

### (*Cup* always means breakfast-cup.)

5 teaspoonfuls - - - = 1 tablespoonful.
2 tablespoonfuls (granulated
    sugar) - - - - = 1 oz.
1 rounded tablespoon
    (butter) - - - = 1 oz.
1 cup of granulated sugar - = ½ lb.
2 cups of flour - - - = 1 pint.
4 cups of flour - - - = 1 lb., or 1 quart.
2½ cups of castor sugar - = 1 lb.
4 tablespoonfuls of coffee
    (dry) - - - - = 1 oz.
1 tablespoonful of coffee
    (liquid) - - - = ½ oz.
10 eggs (without shells) - = 1 lb.
8 eggs (with shells) - - = 1 lb.

# VARIOUS METHODS OF COOKING SUITABLE FOR INVALIDS

*Roasting*, which is done by hanging the meat or poultry before a sharp, open fire, is seldom possible nowadays. It is usually substituted, but not for the better, by :

*Baking*, which is done in the oven—preferably a range oven, but a gas cooker if there is no available range oven. Allow 15 minutes to the pound for red meats, and 20 minutes to the pound for white meats : also allow an extra 15 or 20 minutes for the meat to be well heated through before it begins to be cooked.

For *Boiling*, allow 20 minutes per pound, and an extra 20 minutes. The meat should be put into briskly boiling salted water ; after the first 10 minutes *it must only simmer*, or it will become hard and tough. In almost every case it is preferable to employ—

*Steaming*. Here it is almost essential to have a proper steamer ; but one can manage by using a covered basin which will hold the food to be steamed, and standing this in a pan of *constantly boiling* water. All puddings should be covered with grease-proof paper, well tied down. The old-fashioned pudding-cloth is hardly ever used now. Allow a longer time than for boiling ; *at least* 20 minutes per pound.

*Stewing.*—In this case, meat, or vegetables, or fruit, are cooked in a small amount of liquid, slowly, and for a long while. It must not be confused with re-cooking of already cooked meat ; which is curiously indigestible.

*Frying*—whether wet-frying, when the whole article to be cooked is kept in deep boiling fat, or dry frying, when only a little fat is used in the bottom of the frying pan—is *not advisable* for invalids or convalescents.

*Grilling* is done over a clear fire on a grill or grid iron. Allow 10 to 15 minutes for a half-pound chop or steak. This is suitable for a convalescent : but *fried* chops and steaks, etc., are unwholesome, even for people in good health.

*Braising* is useful for small pieces of meat, such as sweetbreads. But anybody not well acquainted with cooking methods would do better to leave it alone. It really needs a special braising utensil.

## FOOD FOR THE SICK-ROOM: AND OTHER LITTLE MATTERS

THIS is a subject on which I can speak most feelingly : " A pinch of experience is worth a pound of advice," and my pinches of experience have been so frequent, so painful, I am sure they would be totalled up into many pounds ! I don't want to rub in those ordinary first principles of sick-nursing, which can be found in excellent handbooks ; but to offer a few common-sense remarks on what should or should not be done about food for a sick-room ; things only too easy to forget, to ignore, or to be unaware of.

A person, generally speaking, falls ill with little warning : he or she feels unwell, goes to bed, and maybe, remains there for weeks and weeks on end. No preparation, as a rule, is possible : very often the room itself is by no means suitable for a sick-room, but it is a case of Hobson's Choice. To do the best one can with the means in hand, is half the art of life. Anybody who has endured long, wearing illnesses, or short and sharp ones, will bear me out in saying that it's the little things, the little thoughtful attentions, *or the want of them*, which make all the difference. And these are exactly the attentions which one *ought* to get at home, where one is nursed for love and not for money. Never let the patient think you begrudge any care or trouble : do everything as if you were intent on expediting his or her recovery. A cheerful word and a healing touch go a long way : and argument, loud talking inside or outside the room, the bruiting of household difficulties, the report of petty squabbles, must be avoided at all costs. The mind, in illness, is involved just as much as the body ; and worry of any sort is destructive ; too many folks forget this. But the real nurse, who is born and not made, knows that sympathy, tact, and lovingkindness have their own curative power.

One of the chief essentials, as before stated, is absolute punctuality as regards medicines, and meals, if they can be called such. To give the medicines at irregular intervals may prove actually harmful ; to keep the patient waiting for her small allotted food, until she becomes exhausted for want of it, is next door to cruelty. But many people have no sense of time whatever, and " evil is wrought by want of thought as well as want of heart." For these haphazard ones, the only way is to adhere most scrupulously to stated hours by the clock.

Daintiness in serving, as already remarked, is very important. The sick person's fastidious taste will accept what is prettily served, and revolt against a sloppy saucer or bare tray. The tray (covered with a paper tray-cloth) should be removed directly the patient has done with it ; no soiled vessels or utensils of any sort should be allowed to remain in the room : much less scrappy food. This has been said before : but it can't be said too often.

A bottle of good deodoriser-disinfectant is a necessity.

These small matters make a lot of difference —the patient realises that you want her to be pleased, to get better, and that you are not merely satisfied to do things " rather more-or-less."

Light should be kept from falling direct upon the patient's face : this refers less to daylight, which is salutary, than to candles, lamps, gas, etc., which can become extraordinarily annoying. A night-light should be kept going at night, in preference to anything else : it supplies sufficient light, and uses a minimum of air. Gas, turned however low, is devouring the air in the room. Firelight, if the fire has to be kept alight all night, is very soothing and delightful ; but coal should be put on most carefully, lifting each piece in a bit of soft paper. The stoking of the fire in a rough, noisy way can cause actual physical agony to nerves on the raw.

Noise, indeed, is particularly harmful,— noise and fuss of any kind. Creaking shoes are an abomination. The necessary brushing and dusting should be done as quickly and quietly as can be. The smell of cooking should, if possible, be prevented from reaching the sick-room.

Never, for any reason whatever, disturb a patient's sleep : sleep is better than physic or food. But if a feverish person cannot sleep, a cup of tea, in the middle of the night, will often, paradoxically, act as a sedative. The vital strength is at its lowest between 2 and 3 a.m., and the patient feeblest and most restless ; it is the period when a watcher must be extra wary. A cup of good hot tea works wonders then, and the appliances for it should be kept handy. If you haven't a gas-ring, or an electric kettle, procure a spirit-lamp. Milk, and indeed, any kind of food, should be kept outside the room. Coal, and anything likely to be needed at night, should be brought upstairs when the household retires : there should be no hunting after things. Flowers should be removed, especially cut flowers.

Ventilation is a matter of the utmost importance, but you must be careful to keep the patient out of a direct draught ; shift the bed if need be. A fire in the grate creates a certain current of air ; but if the window can be kept open, say four inches at the top, so much the better. (Mind that it doesn't rattle.) Fresh air is healing to an incredible extent ; the old idea of excluding it, resulted in an absolutely poisonous atmosphere.

When washing the patient, let her at least rinse out her mouth, if she isn't strong enough to clean her teeth. This will refresh her greatly, and is very frequently forgotten. Don't worry her about her hair ; simply brush or comb it once a day—plait it, or coil it up, and cover it with a pretty boudoir cap. I wonder more people don't wear these dainty things—they can be made so cheaply and easily out of scraps of lace, odds and ends of soft silk and ribbon. They are very becoming, and make one feel not only tidy, but happy—a vital aid to recovery. A little *négligé* or bed-jacket, with loose-fitting sleeves, is also easily made, and very useful : it is advisable to keep one ready in case of illness. I won't go so far as to emulate the lady in *Dombey and Son*, with her " rose-coloured curtains for doctors," but I am convinced that nobody wants to *look* so ill as she really feels ! Talking of doctors, you should have a clean towel and warm water ready for the doctor to wash his hands. And if you possess a clinical thermometer, and can tell him what the patient's temperature was at morning and evening, it will be most advantageous. The highest temperature of the day is usually present at 6 p.m.

Discreetly dismiss all would-be visitors. They mean well, but they often leave the patient the worse for wear, however much she may think she wants to see them.

Keep the bed and room as neat as you can, but in a quiet, unobtrusive way, without fuss or fidget. Put away the patient's clothes, ready for her recovery : it is a good plan to have them washed, cleaned, mended, etc., while not in use.

The moment that feverishness abates, let the patient be prevented from feeling chilly. A violent perspiration always makes one subsequently cold : and a hot-water bottle, an extra blanket, etc., will probably be wanted. Where faintness occurs, sal volatile sprinkled on a handkerchief is most reviving ; or one teaspoonful of it taken in a wine-glass of tepid water.

Constipation retards recovery more than anything else—except worry. White sugar, white bread, boiled milk are all constipating ; brown bread and brown sugar are the reverse. The effect of fruit varies with individual cases. The doctor should be consulted as to aperients : what suits one person may be bad for another.

Hard cushions placed behind the pillows assist the patient in sitting up when feeble.

Just this word more. "Love," said Henry Drummond, "is the greatest evolutionary force the world has ever known." It is also the greatest recuperative agency. The *desire* to relieve suffering, so characteristic of the Saviour, in itself goes very far to do so. The will must transmute itself into action. It is possible to "make a heaven in hell's despite," even in a sick-room—"a little heaven here below" of love, and sympathy, and thoughtful kindness.

Note.—I have included very few solids, very few cereals ; practically no *fried* anything. (Chops fried are chops ruined.) If there is no griller or gridiron in the house, better cook the chop over a red fire on a toasting-fork. It may be added (lots of people do not know) that the less sugar or sweetstuff one takes the better, because *sweet turns to acid* in the stomach. Bread is better for an invalid if well toasted (not gas-fire toasted), if at a gas-fire, before a sitting-room fire with parallel upright bars : never on a flat grill, which makes the toast hard and indigestible, and the very smell of toast is cheerful for an invalid. Bread and butter should be neatly and thinly cut, not in clumsy chunks. Cakes should be strenuously avoided. Plain, wholesome, *simple* fare is more likely to conduce to recovery for the average person ; the stomach must not be overloaded with unsuitable food.

As regards fruit and vegetables, the doctor's advice must be always taken, because one case varies from another. Therefore few recipes for above are included.

For certain special diseases there are classes of food that possess distinctly curative value : as fresh fruits and vegetables for scurvy, fats and oils in tuberculosis, and pineapple juice in *catarrhal* affections of throat and alimentary canal." For *diabetes*, the whites of two eggs, beaten and mixed with a glass of cold water, are good : if desired, flavoured with lemon juice.

More is to be done for *asthmatic* patients on the side of the stomach, than in any other

25

direction. A cup of very hot water should be taken an hour before each meal, and again at night : but no water should be taken with meals, or until at least 3 hours after. The principal meal should be at midday, and the supper very light. Fats and sweets should be omitted : also pork, veal and rich desserts.

In *chronic rheumatism,* stewed celery is advisable ; also fresh green vegetables, but *not* root crops. No sweet stuffs, as little farinaceous food as possible.

## BEVERAGES

Hot Water
Milk
Tea
Coffee
Beef-Tea
Whole-Beef-Tea
Savoury Beef-Tea
Barley-Water. I
Barley-Water. II
Barley-Water. III
Camomile Tea
Linseed Tea
Suet and Milk
Caudle
Sago Posset
Irish Moss Lemonade
White Wine Whey
Egg Nog

## BEVERAGES

THE best beverage for those not actually ill, but merely out-of-sorts, is plain hot water. Taken an hour before a meal, it swills out the kidneys, and leaves the stomach in a cleaner condition to receive food later on.

The next best, in all probability, is new milk. This does not often agree with people who are eating a lot of meat and so on. But for the average person who is convalescent or elderly, the following is excellent :

One breakfastcupful new milk : let it warm slightly, *but never boil*. (Boiled milk is extremely constipating.) When it is just blood-warm, pour it back into the cup ; with two 5-grain tabloids of sodium citrate, dissolved in a teaspoonful of hot water, which will make the milk agree. Take this in the morning and the evening ; but about an hour before a meal.

The third best is a good cup of tea. Not

everybody knows how to prepare this. It should be made with *freshly boiling* water. Water which *has* boiled, or has been boiling some time, will not brew tea properly. The teapot must be " scalded " first, with the freshly-boiling water. The proper proportion of tea is the old-fashioned one—a teaspoonful per person, and one to the pot. Milk should be put in the cup first, and *no* sugar is the safest rule for everybody. The Chinese, from whom we originally derived our tea, consider us barbarians to adulterate this beautiful drink with milk, and worse than barbarians to spoil it with sugar !

A very excellent blend, which will assist in most cases those miserable headaches of a migraine type, which otherwise yield to nothing—is a special remedial blend, rather expensive, and not for ordinary use—and is made as follows : Take $\frac{1}{2}$ lb. of a *good* Congou blend, not less than 2/8 a pound, 2 oz. of a good China tea, not less than 3/- a pound, and 1 oz. of a good Green tea, not less than 4/6 or 5/- a pound. Mix these thoroughly well, and keep in a closed tin in a dry place.

ISINGLASS AS A STRENGTHENER. A good pinch of Swinborne's Isinglass should be well dissolved in every cup of tea given to an invalid : it has a marked restorative and strengthening effect. One should never be without a packet of Swinborne's Isinglass in the house. It is a wholly different preparation to other gelatinous compounds : and is much more nutritious. This isinglass is a product of the sturgeon.

Coffee is seldom suitable for invalids, but may be very desirable for convalescents, *if properly made*. Four details are essential. (1) Let the coffee be freshly ground, and, if possible, freshly roasted. (2) Do not stint the amount : weak coffee is unendurable. (3) Let the water be *boiling* hot, and all the utensils properly heated. (4) Use only earthenware and wooden utensils : let no metal approach the coffee. Have ready two *well-heated* earthenware jugs, holding about $1\frac{1}{2}$ pints each. Into the first, measure 4 wooden tablespoonfuls (or not less than $2\frac{1}{2}$ oz. per pint) of freshly-ground coffee. Fill up with *boiling* water, stir with spoon, cover with lid ; leave jug in a warm place for 2 or 3 minutes. Stir well once more, let grounds settle, and strain off liquid through butter-muslin into *well-heated* second jug, and serve at once with jug of *boiling* milk. Should any coffee be left over, boil it up along with the milk the second day : it will then be par-ticularly bland and palatable. For those who prefer " French " coffee, i.e. mixed with chicory, it is specially advisable. Any well-known good brand of " French " coffee, such as " Red, White and Blue," can be successfully used according to above direc-tions.

Beef-tea is the usual beverage where others are unsuitable. Properly made, it is of extra-ordinary value. A *real* beef-tea is as " different as chalk from cheese " from shop beef-tea, such as Lemco, Bovril, Oxo, etc. These are excellent, of course, where the housemother doesn't know how to make the other. But plenty of elderly women in their seventies have never known how to make the other, the real stuff; nor have they ever troubled to find out. Many recipes are here appended for beef-tea. It is quite invaluable for a delicate person, if nicely seasoned ; and appeals to a fastidious appetite.

## Beef-Tea. I.

Take 1 lb. gravy beef, remove all fat, pass it through mincer. Place in earthenware jar, with ½ teaspoonful salt and 1 pint cold water. Cover, and tie down with paper. Place in saucepan of boiling water, which must keep simmering 3 hours. Stir contents occasionally. Strain, and remove every trace of grease.

Or, place jar in a very slow oven for 3 hours : stir now and then. Better flavour obtained thus.

Beef-tea *must never boil* : boiling is spoiling.

## Whole - Beef - Tea. II. (*For Convalescents only.*)

Take ½ lb. gravy beef, remove all fat, shred finely. Put in saucepan with ½ pint cold water and ½ teaspoon salt : let soak 15 minutes. Let it begin to heat very slowly ; continue till all the juice is extracted, so that the meat becomes white and the water red-brown. Strain off liquor ; pound meat in mortar. Rub through wire sieve ; add pounded meat to the beef-tea liquor. Very nourishing.

### Savoury Beef-Tea. III.

Take 1 lb. of gravy beef, remove fat, pass through mincer, place in jar with 1 pint cold water, ½ teaspoon salt, small sprig of herbs and parsley, a little piece each of turnip, carrot, onion. Cover, and tie down with paper. Place in pan of boiling water ; simmer very gently for 3 hours. Strain, and remove all grease.

For convalescents only (unless the vegetables are omitted).

### Barley-water. I.

Wash 2 oz. of pearl barley in cold water. Add about 1½ pints of water, a little lemon peel, and sugar to taste. Let it simmer, stirring it often till it is of a nice thickness. Strain, and add lemon juice to taste. A few sweet almonds beaten to a paste will give a pleasant flavour.

### Barley-water. II.

Put 2 oz. pearl barley in a jug, with the thin

rind and juice of a lemon, and a little sugar. Pour in a pint of boiling water ; cover with a clean cloth, let stand till cold, then strain off.

## Another way. III.

Put 2 oz. barley in a clean saucepan, with 2 quarts cold water ; boil till it is reduced to 1 quart. Strain off, and, when cool, add sugar to taste, and flavour with lemon peel or cinnamon.

## Camomile Tea.

Put 1 teaspoonful of dried camomile flowers in a jug with lid, or a jar. Pour 1 cupful (half-pint) boiling water to the flowers, cover, set on side of stove, or in fender : let steep for 15 minutes. Strain off. This is supposed to induce sleep.

## Arrowroot (water).

Mix 1 dessertspoonful (or 2 teaspoonfuls) of the best Bermuda arrowroot, with a very little cold water, enough to make a thick paste, in a breakfast-cup. Pour on (stirring all the time), boiling water to fill the cup. Sweeten to taste.

A little cinnamon (in case of diarrhœa) or 2 or 3 drops of ginger essence, may be added. Some people put the mixed paste to the boiling water (1 breakfastcupful), in a saucepan, and boil it for 10 minutes. Arrowroot can also be made with milk : but this is too heavy for many persons.

## Black Currant Tea.

Put a heaped tablespoonful of black currant jam into a jug ; pour in half a pint of boiling water. Stir well, cover up with a folded cloth. Let stand till nearly cold, then strain off into another jug.

## Linseed Tea.

To 1 tablespoonful of linseed, add 2 breakfastcupfuls of cold water. Place in a clean pan : bring to boiling, let boil for 30 to 35 minutes. Strain off, sweeten to taste with honey or sugar as preferred, and put in the juice of one lemon.

## Suet and Milk.

Have an ounce of fresh suet, finely grated, tied up in a muslin bag, and simmered for

30 minutes in a quart of new milk. Add sugar to taste, and any flavouring that is liked.

### Caudle.

Whisk an egg till it froths ; stir into this a cup of very smooth and very hot gruel. Add 1 teaspoonful of sugar, grated nutmeg to taste, and half a cupful of sherry.

### Sago Posset.

Boil 3 oz. of sago in a quart of water till a mucilage is formed. Rub half an ounce of loaf sugar on the rind of a lemon, and put it, with a teaspoonful of ginger essence, into half a pint of sherry. Add to this the sago mucilage, and boil the whole for 5 minutes. This is an excellent cordial, where acute diseases (not of an inflammatory kind) have left the patient in a state of debility. A little may be taken at a time, every 4 or 5 hours.


### Irish Moss Lemonade.

Pick over ¼ cupful of Irish Moss, pour over it enough cold water to cover it. Then drain away the water, add a pint of fresh water, and let cook 20 minutes in a double-boiler, then strain. To $\frac{1}{2}$ a cup of the liquid, add the juice of 1 lemon, and sugar to taste.

## White Wine Whey.

Heat 1 pint milk to boiling point : add the juice of $\frac{1}{2}$ a lemon, free of seeds : let milk come again to boiling point : then strain the whey through a cheese-cloth without pressure. Add $\frac{1}{2}$ a cup of light sherry. Useful as a beverage in feverish diseases : promotes perspiration.

## Egg Nog.

Beat well 1 egg-yolk : add 1 or 2 teaspoonfuls sugar : mix sugar in the yolk : add 1 tablespoonful sherry or brandy, then add, gradually, 1 cupful milk. Lastly, fold in the white of egg, beaten stiff.

## SALT DISHES

Barley Cream
Beef Jelly
Grilled Chop
" Salisbury " Minced Beef
Chicken Panada
Chicken Purée
Veal Broth
Savoury Custard
French Omelet
Puffy Omelet
Chicken Custard
Sweetbreads  (Stewed)
Sweetbreads  (Fried)
Stewed Lamb's Sweetbreads
Stewed Tripe
Steamed Fish
Fish Souffle
Filleted Plaice
Steamed Dried Haddock
Baked Sole
Baked Whiting
Cheese Toast
Cheese Pudding
Cheese Straws

# SALT DISHES

## Barley Cream (*Nutritious and Digestible*).

Take ½ lb. of chicken, or of veal cutlet : pass through mincer. Wash and blanch ½ oz. pearl barley. Put into saucepan with ½ pint cold water, and a little salt. Bring to boil, then let simmer gently for 2 hours. Pound meat and barley in a mortar with a little of juice : season, rub through sieve : add cream slightly whipped, and warm up if required hot.

## Beef Jelly.

Take a small knuckle of veal, break it into small pieces, and let it soak 2 hours in 2 pints of cold water. Then boil it till reduced to a pint. Strain it. Take 1 lb. of lean beef, remove all skin and fat, and scrape or finely mince it. Let it stand in a jar in 1 pint of cold water for 1 hour. Then cover the jar and put it in a saucepan of cold water, and let it warm very slowly till it simmers. Then strain it, add the veal stock and a little pepper and salt, and pour off into a mould to cool.

### Grilled Chop.

Have a clear, red fire—hot, but not fierce. Take a lamb or mutton chop, season it with salt and pepper. Brush the gridiron with a little butter : cook for 4 minutes on each side, or until juice begins to drop black. Mix a tiny pat of butter with a little chopped parsley and lemon juice : place on chop, serve at once.

### " Salisbury " Minced Beef.

1 lb. lean rump steak (this suffices for two meals). Remove all fat, skin, and gristle. Put it three times through a mincer, and then into a small saucepan, with just enough water to cover it : but don't make it too liquid. When it turns from red to brown (simmering slowly and *never coming anywhere near boiling*), it is done enough. Serve some in a hot soup-dish, with bread, bread and butter, or sippets of toast. The remainder can be reheated once, *but not twice* : if any is left the second

time it must be eaten cold. To beat it with a
fork while cooking, improves it. It is essential
that it *only just turns colour*: if it boils, it
becomes hard and is ruined.

## Chicken Panada.

Cut up the meat from which chicken-broth
has been made : pound it in a mortar, or beat
it with a rolling-pin. Put it in a pan on the
fire, with a little milk and salt. Stir it, until
heated through, *but don't let it boil.* Add a few
breadcrumbs to thicken it : stir in one
slightly beaten egg to each quarter of a fowl.
It may be used either as spoon meat when hot,
or made into little balls and served in the
chicken broth. Will keep good for some days.

## Chicken Purée.

Take the remains of a cold roast fowl ;
pound up the flesh with a little white sauce :
sieve it. Heat it up with a little cream, and
serve it in a border of rice.

## Veal Broth.

Put into a basin 1 oz. of pearl barley or of
sago : pour some lukewarm water over, and

let it soak a few minutes : have ready, cut up small, and the skin removed, 1 lb. of lean veal (leg or knuckle), place it in a casserole with a pinch of salt and 2 pints of cold water. Bring slowly to boiling, skim off any fat, let simmer slowly for 2 to 3 hours. Add the soaked barley or sago, and in ½ hour take up broth, strain it into a clean saucepan. Have 1 beaten yolk of egg, mixed with ½ gill of milk, stirred into broth ; add seasoning of salt and pepper. Mix well, reheat, serve hot. Mutton (lean) may be prepared the same way.

### Savoury Custard.

To the beaten yolks of 2 eggs, add a pinch of salt, a tiny dash of pepper, and a cup of good, strong beef-tea or mutton broth, from which all fat has been carefully removed. Pour into a small buttered basin, and poach in a pan or dish of hot water, until the custard is set. Serve in the basin.

### French Omelet.

Take 2 eggs, 2 extra yolks, 3 tablespoonfuls of water, a pinch of salt. Beat all together with a fork until you can take up a spoonful smooth. Have 1 tablespoonful of butter just melted, in a clean, smooth, thin pan. Pour in the batter ; place the pan over heat for a moment to let the batter set. Then take a thin knife, separate the set part from the sides of the pan, and keep on gently rocking the pan to and from you, so that the liquid part may run to the hot pan. When it is all creamy, roll it over, beginning at the handle side of the pan, and let it brown a minute or two on the hot stove. Then place on a hot dish and serve immediately. Omelets of all kinds are ruined if " kept hot " for any time.

## Puffy Omelet.

Beat 2 yolks till they are thick ; beat 2 whites till they are stiff. Add a pinch of salt to the yolks, and 1 tablespoonful of water for each yolk. Mix well, then place yolks on beaten white, and cut and fold the whites into the yolks. Have 1 tablespoonful of butter melted in a hot pan : spread the batter evenly in. Let stand about 2 minutes over a moderate heat : then put the pan into the oven to brown over the top slightly. When a sharp knife thrust into the centre of the omelet will come out nearly clean, take the pan out of oven, cut the omelet across the centre of top (*but not right through*), at right-angles to the handle; fold the part nearest handle over the other part, slip on to hot dish, and serve at once.

### Chicken Custard (*for Convalescents*).

Place in a buttered basin a teacupful of fine bread-crumbs from a stale loaf; the same amount of chicken-breast, finely chopped; a beaten egg; a pinch of celery salt, and half a breakfastcupful of milk, or a little more if need be. Mix thoroughly; poach in hot water, or cook in slow oven. Serve hot.

### Sweetbreads (Stewed).

These are more digestible than fried sweet-breads. Soak 2 in cold water for 1 hour. Put into boiling water, boil for 10 minutes: then place in cold water for 20 minutes. Put them in a stewpan, with pepper, salt, and powdered mace to taste: cover with a cupful and a half of good white stock. When they have simmered gently for 30 to 45 minutes, take them out of the pan, and keep them hot, while you thicken the gravy with flour and butter, bring it to the boil, and add 4 table-spoonfuls of cream or milk. Pour it over the sweetbreads on a hot dish, and serve with cut lemon.

## Sweetbreads (Fried.)

Take 2 lambs' throat sweetbreads. Blanch them by putting into a pan of cold water. Bring to boiling, simmer gently for 3 minutes. This will make them white and firm. Remove all fat and gristle, but not the skin. Brush with a well-beaten egg, seasoned with salt and pepper. Dip in bread-crumbs, which should be flattened-on with a knife. Place in a small pan with $\frac{1}{2}$ oz. of butter : fry to a golden-brown. Drain, and serve on a dish-paper garnished with parsley.

## Stewed Lamb's Sweetbreads.

Take $\frac{1}{2}$ lb. lamb's sweetbreads, place in earthenware casserole : just cover them with cold water. Let boil for 3 minutes. Strain them out, and put them into cold water.

Remove all skin and fat ; wash out casserole, put back the sweetbreads in it, with a teacupful white stock ; add sweetbreads, with a little celery salt, and a pinch of pepper. Cover casserole, let simmer slowly for $\frac{3}{4}$ to 1 hour until sweetbread is tender. Mix teaspoonful cornflour to smooth paste, with a little cold water. Let soak a few minutes more. Add 1 teaspoonful minced parsley, and 1 tablespoonful cream, just before it is served.

### Stewed Tripe.

Take $\frac{1}{2}$ lb. dressed tripe. Wash it well and cut it up in little pieces. Place it in an earthenware casserole with just enough cold water to cover it. Let it boil ; strain off the water, add 1 teacupful milk : let stew very slowly until tender. A little thinly-sliced onion can be added at pleasure. When the tripe is thoroughly tender, mix 1 teaspoonful flour with a little water into a smooth paste : add to the tripe, stir until well blended. Add $\frac{1}{2}$ oz. butter, season with salt and pepper to taste : let cook a little longer, and serve very hot. Dry toast should accompany it.

## Steamed Fish (Sole, whiting or haddock).

Fillet if possible. Place in lightly-buttered soup-plate, sprinkle with lemon juice, pepper and salt : cover with buttered paper : place another plate over it. Put it on top of a saucepan half full of boiling water, which must boil for about 30 minutes. If they are thick fillets, or a whole fish, turn once. When fish looks thick and white, no longer transparent, it is cooked. Serve with white or parsley sauce, or simply with its own juice poured round. This is the lightest and most digestible method.

Can also be done in oven the same way ; 10 minutes to $\frac{1}{2}$ hour, according to size.

## Fish Soufflé.

Take a plaice, about $1\frac{1}{2}$ lb. ; clean and steam. Remove skin and bones, and pound the flesh, along with a little butter, till it can be rubbed through a sieve into a bowl. Mix 3 beaten yolks with it, and subsequently 3 whites whisked stiff. Place in small cups or bowls, cook in a moderate oven for 10 minutes. Serve very hot.

## Filleted Plaice.

Choose a nice plaice, have it filleted : place the fillets on a buttered plate, with a little pepper, salt and lemon juice sprinkled over them. Cover up with another buttered plate, and cook over a pan of boiling water for about 10 or 12 minutes.

## Steamed Dried Haddock.

(A London doctor told me that this was the most wholesome, if not the only wholesome way, he had ever heard of preparing dried haddock. It is not uncommon at coroner's inquests to hear of a death taking place after eating dried haddock, because it has been rendered tough and indigestible by people *cooking* it, whereas it is already cooked in the process of drying. But, if done the following way, the doctor said he could recommend it to a delicate patient.)

Take a medium-sized finnan haddock, or a piece of a large one : remove fins and head : place it in an earthenware bowl : pour *boiling* water over so as to cover it completely : put a thick folded cloth over bowl so as to retain all steam and heat : stand on top of oven, or in a similarly warm place, for about 15 minutes. Then strain off all water : lift fish on to a *hot* dish : strew a little butter on : serve at once. The flesh will now be found tender and appetising.

## Baked Sole.

Take 1 filleted sole, wipe and trim the fillets : dust them with a little pepper and salt, double them over, place them in a lightly buttered shallow casserole. Put in 2 tablespoonfuls cold water and a little lemon juice. Cover with buttered paper, tied firmly. Place in a moderate oven for about 12 minutes. Serve with cut lemon and bread and butter.

## Baked Whiting.

Have a whiting skinned and cleaned, put it in a buttered pie-dish, add salt and pepper to taste, and a squeeze of lemon juice. Have 1 gill of milk and water (half-and-half) made hot but not quite boiling ; pour this over the fish and set the dish in a quick oven for a quarter of an hour. Baste often.

### Cheese Toast.

(Very wholesome and appetising, if served at once and *not allowed to set hard*.)

Grate some dry Cheddar cheese, about a breakfastcupful. Place this in a small basin, pour boiling water on, enough to cover cheese : put a clean cloth over basin, stand it on top of stove for 10 to 15 minutes. Meanwhile have ready a nice square (without crust) of buttered toast, kept hot. Strain off all liquid from basin, spread cheese on toast, and serve at once, with salt and pepper.

### Cheese Pudding.

About 1 breakfastcupful grated Cheddar or Gruyère : beat up 2 fresh eggs ; mix cheese in, with seasoning to taste. Add a breakfastcupful milk : strew some shreds of butter on top, and bake in moderate oven. Do not let the oven get too hot, lest the egg should curdle.

### Cheese Straws.

$2\frac{1}{2}$ oz. grated cheese, 2 oz. flour, 2 oz. butter, pepper and salt to taste, and (at pleasure) an eggspoonful dry mustard : add 1 well-beaten egg, and 1 tablespoonful cold water. Mix well : flour a pasteboard, roll out the cheese paste, cut it in thin strips, and bake in a buttered tin for 20 minutes, or until it is a golden brown.

# GRUEL, PORRIDGE, AND SUCH-LIKE

NOTE.—I don't include many of these recipes, because some people can't digest them, some thoroughly dislike them, and some are averse from all cereal preparations. Porridge made with plain water is lighter and more wholesome for most invalids than porridge made with milk. The latter can be added later. Salt seasoning is preferable to sweet seasoning, especially for Irish and Scottish folk. In any case, *thorough* cooking of oatmeal is necessary, otherwise the oatmeal continues to expand inside one, causing great flatulence and discomfort. Some people cook Scott's Porage Oats overnight and then reheat it next morning to make sure of it being thoroughly expanded.

## Oatmeal Gruel.

Sprinkle 1 cupful of Scotch oatmeal into 2 quarts of boiling water (salted). Let cook in a double-boiler for 3 hours, then strain through cheese cloth. Sweeten or use salt according to taste. The gruel should be diluted by adding, to a half-cupful, half a cupful of thin cream, and about 1 pint of boiling water, unless it is preferred thicker.

# VEGETABLE DISHES

**Artichoke Soufflé**
**Cauliflower Purée**
**Sea-Kale**
**Turnip-Tops**

# VEGETABLE DISHES

## Artichoke Soufflé.

Take some Jerusalem artichokes (probably a pound would suffice), wash and clean well, boil in salted water until soft enough to press through a sieve. Season with salt and pepper. Have ready a custard made with 2 beaten yolks and a cupful of milk : then add 2 whisked whites : mix with the sieved artichoke, pour all into a mould, and steam for 1 hour. Very digestible and nourishing.

## Cauliflower Purée.

Take a good, fresh, large white head of cauliflower. Remove outer leaves, wash thoroughly, but do not cut off stalk. Place in a saucepan with 3 quarts of water, half-cupful milk, and a teaspoonful salt. Let boil for 50 minutes. Remove, drain well, then rub through a sieve into a smaller saucepan. Add

1 oz. good butter, 2 saltspoonfuls salt, 1 salt-spoonful each of grated nutmeg and of white pepper. Mix thoroughly whilst reheating for 5 minutes. Serve in heated dish or soup plate.

## Sea-Kale.

Wash the sea-kale well, tie it into small bundles like asparagus, but leave enough of the main stump to prevent the branches falling apart. Put into boiling salted water, just enough to cover it ; boil until tender, say 25 to 30 minutes. Remove, drain, unloose the bundles, and serve on buttered toast in a hot dish. White sauce or thickened gravy may be poured over it, but this is liable to muffle the peculiar flavour of the sea-kale, which is delicate and nutritious, and makes a nice change.

## Turnip-Tops.

Excellent as a purifier of the blood after any inflammatory fever. Take some quite young turnip-tops, have them well washed and picked, cook them (like spinach) in their own moisture or in the least possible quantity of boiling salted water. About 15 to 20 minutes should suffice. Drain them thoroughly, pressing out the wetness : chop them small with a sharp knife, mix a little butter in, and serve very hot.

# SWEET DISHES

Apple Snow
Arrowroot Blancmange
Arrowroot Jelly
Lemon Sponge
Biscuit Pudding
Boiled Batter Pudding
Junket. I
Junket. II
Friar's Omelet
Marrow Pudding for Invalids
Jaunemange
Isinglass Blancmange
Irish Moss Blancmange
Jellies
Fruit Dishes

# SWEET DISHES

## Apple Snow.

Peel, core, quarter 3 apples. Place in saucepan with 2 tablespoonfuls cold water, and thin strip lemon peel. Stew till soft, remove lemon peel, beat apples to a pulp. Have 1 white of egg whisked very stiff; lightly stir in the apple-pulp, and 1 tablespoonful castor sugar. Whisk till stiff; place in glass dish.

## Arrowroot Blancmange.

Boil 1 pint milk, with sugar and vanilla (or cinnamon) flavouring to taste. Blend a tablespoonful of good Bermuda arrowroot into a paste with a little cold milk: pour this into the boiling milk, stir till it is perfectly smooth, boil for a few minutes, pour into a wetted mould: set in cool place.

## Arrowroot Jelly.

Pound 3 bitter almonds: thinly peel a

lemon : put all into a large wineglassful of water, and let steep for 4 or 5 hours. Then strain the liquid, mix it smooth with 4 table-spoonfuls of arrowroot, an equal quantity of lemon juice, 2 tablespoonfuls of brandy, and sugar to taste. Stir this over the fire till it becomes quite thick. Remove from fire, and when it cools, pour into small jelly glasses, and set by in a cool place.

**Lemon Sponge.**

Put into saucepan $\frac{1}{2}$ pint water, $\frac{1}{2}$ oz. sheet-gelatine, thin rind of 1 lemon, 1 oz. sugar. Heat until gelatine is thoroughly dissolved. Have white of 1 egg and juice of 1 lemon in a large bowl ; strain in the hot liquid : whisk all together until stiff. Pile in heaps in glass dish, or pour into a mould (cold-water-rinsed), and turn out when set firm.

**Biscuit Pudding.**

Place in a basin 2 eggs and 3 oz. castor sugar. Whisk to a thick, creamy froth. Lightly stir in (with a metal spoon) 3 oz. ground rice, $\frac{1}{2}$ teaspoonful baking-powder, a few drops of vanilla. Have some small dariole moulds or little tins, filled three-quarters full with mixture ; bake 20 minutes, serve with jam sauce. (Convalescents only.)

## Boiled Batter Pudding.

Sift into a basin 4 oz. flour and $\frac{1}{2}$ teaspoonful salt. Add 2 beaten eggs, stir in gradually $\frac{1}{2}$ pint milk. Beat well : let stand 20 minutes. Pour into well-buttered pudding-basin : scald and flour cloth, tie over : boil 1 hour. Serve with sweet sauce or castor sugar.

## Junket. I.

Heat 1 pint milk to 98°. Put it in a glass bowl : add 1 teaspoonful sugar and junket powder (as indicated on packet) or 1 tablespoonful rennet essence. Let stand without moving, for $1\frac{1}{2}$ hours in warmish place. Very nutritious, refreshing, and digestible.

## Junket. II.

Heat 1 breakfastcupful new milk until it is lukewarm : put in 1 tablespoonful of sugar. When the sugar is dissolved, stir in 1 teaspoonful of liquid rennet, and $\frac{1}{2}$ tablespoonful of brandy. (The last can be omitted except in

67

cases of great weakness.)  Pour off at once into small bowls. Stand them in a warm place till well set : then stand in a cool place. A little nutmeg can be grated over top.

## Friar's Omelet.

Stew 4 apples with 2 oz. sugar, 1 oz. butter, grated rind and juice of $\frac{1}{2}$ lemon, till quite smooth. Remove from fire, stir in 1 well-beaten egg. Put 1 oz. breadcrumbs at bottom of pie dish, pour in the mixture, cover with equal quantity crumbs and sprinkle with minute bits of butter, bake 15 minutes.

## Marrow Pudding for Invalids.

Take 4 oz. good beef marrow (chopped), 4 oz. fine bread-crumbs, 8 oz. chopped figs, about 2 oz. flour, a pinch of salt. Mix with a little milk or water, place in a buttered basin, boil for 3 hours, or steam for longer.

## Jaunemange.

Put 1 oz. of Swinborne's isinglass into a jar or basin, with a large lemon rind cut very thinly. Pour 1 breakfastcupful cold water on it : let stand at least 10 minutes. Then add

4 oz. loaf sugar, the juice of 1½ lemons, 1 tablespoonful brandy, 1 wineglassful sherry. If no sherry is added, put a little more cold water, ½ pint of boiling water, and 4 fresh yolks, well beaten. Mix all very well, taking care that the yolks do not " break." Stand the jar in a pan of boiling water, and let the contents just *nearly* come to boiling. It needs careful stirring and attention. When the ingredients are quite dissolved, take out the lemon. Lift out the jar of jaunemange, and stand it in a bowl of cold water to set. Or pour it off, when a little cool, into a mould. This preparation is extremely nourishing and strengthening ; it can be taken at any time, a few teaspoonfuls being sufficient. It is so pleasant to the taste, and so unlike anything else, that the most fastidious invalid will hardly refuse it. In cases involving diarrhœa, the lemon juice should be omitted.

## Isinglass Blancmange.

Take 1 oz. Swinborne's isinglass ; soak a third of packet in 1 breakfastcupful new milk, for a few minutes. Pour into a small saucepan, bring to the boil, stirring with a fork to assist the isinglass in dissolving. Boil for, say, 2 minutes ; pour off into a small bowl : add 1 teaspoonful sugar, and 2 or 3 drops lemon essence. Stir in well, and stand in a cool place till it sets cold. This may take several hours, according to temperature of weather.

### Irish Moss Blancmange.

Irish Moss ("Carrageen") can be bought by the packet from any chemist. A small amount should be soaked in luke-warm water for 30 minutes, then strained off, and any black or discoloured bits of seaweed removed. It should next be put into a double boiler with new milk, and let cook slowly, for at least two hours. Strain, add a little cream, sugar, and vanilla essence. Bring to the boil, stirring frequently ; pour off into a small, cold-water-wetted mould ; let set cold and firm, and turn out. A spoonful or two at a time will be found beneficial.

## JELLIES

Apple Jelly
Arrowroot Jelly
Beef-Tea Jelly
Calf's-Foot Jelly
Claret Jelly
Egg Jelly
Invalid Jelly.  I
Invalid Jelly.  II
Linseed Jelly
Meat Jelly for Invalids
Mutton Jelly
Nourishing Jelly
Restorative Jelly
Rose Jelly

# JELLIES

### Linseed Jelly.

Put 1 lb. linseed into 2 quarts water : bring to boiling, let simmer for 3 hours ; strain off. Pour liquid back into saucepan, with 4 oz. Valentia raisins, and the pulp of a large lemon. Let simmer, but not boil, for an hour longer : then strain again, and add sugar to taste (probably $\frac{1}{2}$ lb.).

### Beef-Tea Jelly.

Make $\frac{1}{2}$ pint good beef-tea, strain into basin. Melt 1 oz. gelatine in 2 tablespoonfuls water in a saucepan : strain this into beef-tea. Season, set in small moulds to set. When firm, turn out, or serve in moulds. Handy when people are fed-up with beef-tea.

### Apple Jelly.

1 lb. apples, peeled and sliced ; place in saucepan with thin rind and juice of 1 lemon,

½ pint water, 3 oz. castor sugar.  Simmer till tender : rub through hair sieve.  Melt ½ oz. sheet gelatine in ½ gill warm water, strain into the rest.  Pour into dariole moulds, rinsed with cold water.  When set, dip into warm water, and turn on to glass dish.

### Egg Jelly.

Rub 6 oz. loaf sugar upon 2 lemons, squeeze out juice, make up to 1 pint with water. Beat 2 eggs ; put all into saucepan, with 1 oz. sheet gelatine.  Whisk till almost boiling, but don't let boil.  Strain, pour into little (cold-water-rinsed) moulds.  When set firm, turn out on cold dish as above.  Nourishing, tempting, refreshing.

### Arrowroot Jelly.

Place in a cup 2 heaped teaspoonfuls of the best arrowroot : mix into a paste, with just enough cold water : add a pinch of salt. Pour boiling water up to rim of cup : turn into saucepan, boil till transparent.  Flavour with a little cinnamon, or (in fever cases) the juice of a quarter-lemon, and sugar to taste.

### Invalid Jelly.  I.

Mix to a paste, with a little cold water, 1 heaped tablespoonful arrowroot. Add 1 well-whisked egg, 3 tablespoonfuls granulated sugar, the juice and grated rind of a lemon. Mix thoroughly ; stir in enough boiling water to make 1 pint ; place in saucepan, boil for 2 or 3 minutes. Pour off into dish ; let grow cold, then mask with whipped cream.

### Invalid Jelly.  II.

Take ½ lb. each of good rump steak, of veal, and of mutton ; remove all fat, cut up small, place in earthen jar with 2 tablespoonfuls water and a pinch of salt. Cover closely, steam for 6 hours ; then strain off and pour into small shapes, previously wetted with cold water.

### Restorative Jelly.

Dissolve 1 oz. of isinglass in 1 quart of water, let it simmer gently till reduced to a pint, then add ½ lb. of fine loaf sugar. When dissolved, strain it off, and put it into a pudding-dish in the cellar till cold. To be taken in the quantity necessary to sweeten any liquid such as tea, etc.

### Calf's-Foot Jelly (Sweet).

Take 4 calves' feet, divide and wash them : remove all fat ; place them in a pan with 3 pints cold water. Let them come to boil slowly, skimming well : then let simmer very slowly for 6 hours. Strain off through sieve, leave for 12 hours, and remove fat. (It should be stiff by then ; if not, a little isinglass must be added.) Place 1 quart of this stock in a pan, with the rind and juice of 3 lemons, 6 oz. sugar, 2 cloves, and a small teaspoonful powdered cinnamon. Beat the whites and shells of 2 eggs in 2 tablespoonfuls water, and put to the rest. Stir now and then. When the jelly boils, let it reach the top of the pan ; then draw aside. Leave it for 10 minutes. Have ready a cheese-cloth jelly-bag, scald it by pouring through it 1 quart boiling water. Then strain the jelly through (it can be strained twice if not clear enough), and put it into small glasses or moulds.

### Claret Jelly.

Put into a clean saucepan 10 oz. lump sugar, 1 oz. gelatine, the juice and thin rind of 1 lemon, the contents of a small pot of red-currant jelly, and a bottle of Australian claret. Bring to boil gently ; let boil 3 minutes, move to side of stove for 20 minutes. Let cool, pour into wetted mould, let stand till next day.

### Mutton Jelly.

Cut into small pieces 1 lb. of lean veal : add 1 lb, neck of mutton (scrag end), and a teacupful of pearl barley, well washed. Place in a pan, with a quart of cold water. Let simmer gently all day long. Add a pinch of salt when done ; strain, and pour off to go cold until next day.

### Nourishing Jelly.

Cut up in small pieces, 2 lb. gravy beef, 2 lb. to 3 lb. knuckle of veal, 1 calf's foot. Place in a clean saucepan, with just enough cold water to cover meat. Put in 1 tea-spoonful salt, 4 cloves, 1 bay-leaf, $\frac{1}{2}$ teaspoonful powdered mace, and a few peppercorns. Let the stock come to boiling very slowly ; skim it often. When it boils, let it simmer beside a slow fire for *at least* 8 hours, often giving it a good stir. It should be strained through a hair sieve and set to cool ; next day remove every atom of fat.

### Rose Jelly.

Rub 8 oz. loaf sugar upon the rind of a good sized lemon : boil this in 1 pint of new milk. When it is quite cold, add the strained juice of the lemon, 1 wineglassful of sherry or Marsala, ½ oz. gelatine dissolved in a little cold water, and a few drops of cochineal. Stir this into the milk ; place it in a wetted mould. Turn out when set, and serve with whipped cream.

### Meat Jelly for Invalids.

Place in a jar, without any water, 1 lb. of shin of beef, cut up rather small : 1 lb. of lean veal, also cut up : 1 smallish chicken, disjointed and well cleaned. Put the jar in boiling water, in a saucepan (or a double boiler) on the hob, until the juice is all extracted. Season to taste, let stand till it becomes a jelly. This is particularly strengthening.

## FRUIT DISHES

**Baked Apples**
**Grape-Fruit**
**Oranges and Lemons**
**Scraped Apples**
**Pine-apples**

.

# FRUIT DISHES

## Baked Apples.

Take 2 or 3 large, sound cooking apples,
such as Bramley's Seedlings : wipe them well,
and cut a ring all round them. Bake in a
slightly buttered tin, in a good oven, until
done. The ring facilitates the cooking, and
makes the apples much softer. (This is a
hospital recipe.)

## Grape-Fruit.

No doubt good, ripe, fresh grape-fruit are
the best for one ; but many invalids find them
rather a bother to eat. A really good brand
of tinned grape-fruit, *not too cheap*, is then
preferable ; and, if taken for supper, has
a tendency to promote a free action of the
bowels next morning.

## Oranges and Lemons.

Oranges do not always agree with every-
one ; in some cases they induce a slight

biliousness.   Lemons, just plain lemons, *when the patient can take them*, are excellent, especially for rheumatic persons.   Lemons are, however, an acquired taste : and many people would find them impossibly sour.

### Scraped Apples.

Sweet eating apples, peeled and scraped into a glass dish, and some custard then poured over them (when it has cooled off a little) will tempt the appetite of a sick child, and be very wholesome for it.   I mean real custard, which is made with eggs ; powdered custard is not.

### Pine-apples.

The pine-apple is the only fruit which is known materially to aid digestion.   If eaten fresh, and without sugar, its beneficial effects can hardly be over-estimated.

Lightning Source UK Ltd.
Milton Keynes UK
UKHW012001060921
390129UK00002B/633